D0479760

An Enlightened Life

Author : Kieron Moore

Illustrator : Rajesh Nagulakonda

Colorists : Rajesh Nagulakonda
Pradeep Sherawat

Editor : Sourav Dutta

Letterer : Bhavnath Chaudhary

www.campfire.co.in

Published by Kalyani Navyug Media Pvt Ltd
101 C, Shiv House, Hari Nagar Ashram,
New Delhi 110014, India

ISBN: 978-93-81182-29-1

Printed in India

BUDDHA

An Enlightened Life

KALYANI NAVYUG MEDIA PVT LTD

PRELUDE
Once upon a time...
Once there was a greedy Crane, a pond full of Fish, and a summer when no rain fell.
Poor Fish are running out of water! I know of a pond deep in the woods – let me take you there.
The Fish did not believe the Crane, but one brave Fish volunteered to go.
What a magnificent pond! Take me back so I can tell everyone you are a truthful Crane.
When they heard of the pond, all the Fish wanted to be taken there.
The pond is cool and shady, and much larger than ours.
The Crane offered to take all the Fish – one at a time.
But he took the Fish into the woods, where he put them down and ate them.
Soon, the Crane had eaten all the Fish from the pond.

These are some of the many incarnations of the Buddha before he lived no more.

But first, there was a Queen who had a dream...

1 PRINCE SIDDHARTHA

'They dressed me in the most heavenly of cloths and adorned me with divine flowers.'
'I was approached by a white elephant, with six magnificent tusks and a lotus flower in its trunk.'
'And then, after circling me five times...'

...the elephant entered my womb, from the right-hand side.
Incredible! What an incredible dream.

What does this mean, Master Asita?

It means, Your Majesty, that Queen Maya will soon give birth to the Purest One, a child who will become very great indeed.

Remarkable news! My son will be a powerful King! Even more powerful than me!

And so, as Queen Maya waited for her child to be born, the city of Kapilavastu, capital of the Shakya clan, eagerly awaited the arrival of the new Prince.

When the time came to give birth, the Queen set out to her parents' house, as was the custom.
On the way, they passed the beautiful Lumbini Park.
Stop here. I need to rest.

But it was in this park, on the night of a full moon, that Queen Maya gave birth.

Look at you. My baby Prince. You'll grow up to be a King, you know that?

The Queen returned at once to Kapilavastu, though a fierce illness was creeping up on her.
Are you all right, Your Majesty? You look terribly pale. We could rest some more.
We will carry on. My Prince must see his palace.

King Suddhodana was most pleased with his new son, and invited nine wise men to help choose a name.
What about Siddhartha?

Siddhartha... I like it.
Tell me, what will my Prince Siddhartha grow up to be?

This Prince will grow up to be a Chakravarti, a King of Kings.
Yes. He will walk through the skies and rule over the whole world.

No, no, no. This Prince will become a wise spiritual ruler – a Buddha.

What? You can't be sure of this, Kondanna?
I am certain, he will renounce the noble life in order to end suffering.

What do you say, Master Asita?
Hmm... This Prince could become King of Kings if he wishes to rule. But should he choose a religious life... Yes, he could just as likely become a Buddha.

But what would become of my kingdom?
Your Majesty! It's the Queen, she's fallen horribly ill!

Maya, my love, you stay strong. You can make it through this.

I don't think so... I'm afraid my time is up. Now, tell me about our son.

Your Majesty, is the Queen...

The Queen is dead.

I must take Siddhartha away from her. And one more thing...

But each palace was equally a prison. Siddhartha came to realize something was being kept from him, and longed to travel outside the palace gates.

Siddhartha was a compassionate child, a quality not shared by his cousin Devadatta...
Look! What a wonderful swan!
Watch me hit it!
No!
THUNK
You hurt it!
What are you doing?
I'm helping the poor bird.

Get off it, it's mine!
It's a living creature!
I shot it, that makes it mine! Anyone knows that's how it works!
Oh, really? Let's go and ask Master Asita, then!
Master Asita, I shot this bird, so...
You wounded it! It's still...
That doesn't matter! It's mine...
Then why was I the one who helped...
Enough!
A life can never belong to one who tries to destroy it, but only to one who tries to save it. Therefore, the swan belongs not to Devadatta, but to Siddhartha.
Huh. Not fair!

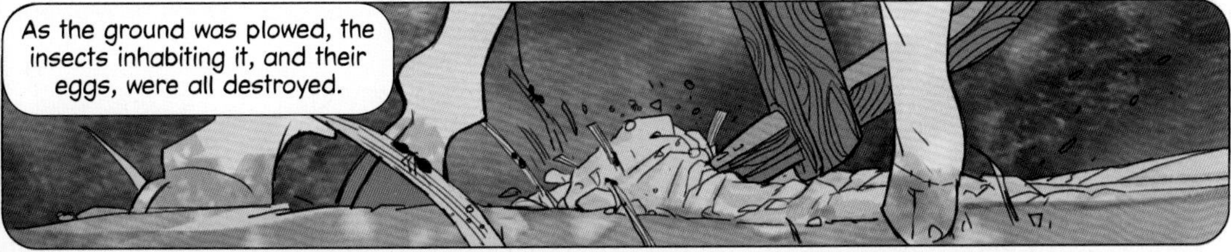

It was carnage, and it filled Siddhartha with a deep sorrow, as if every individual ant were a close friend of his.

But then, from that sorrow...

When Suddhodana returned, he saw his son remained under the tree's shadow, though the other shadows had moved on.

As he watched Siddhartha grow up, Suddhodana noticed the longing to escape the palace grow within his son.
I worry about the boy, Asita. He wanders around all day.
Your son is depressed. Maybe some company would cheer him up?
Where are you taking me, Father?
I have a surprise for you, Siddhartha.
The most heavenly girls of the Shakya lands - choose one to be your bride!
Greetings. I'm Siddhartha.
My Prince, I am Yasodhara.

Soon, Suddhodana had his son's new bride brought to his courtroom.

Your Majesty. How may I help you?

You're very beautiful, Yasodhara. You will make a fine bride for the Prince. Just what he needs. Walk with me.

You see, Yasodhara, my son has a habit of... being overly concerned about small matters. You can play a part in helping him overcome this.

I will see to it that you have a magnificent wedding, and in return you will see to it that Siddhartha remains where he cannot be upset.

You wish me to keep him from leaving the palaces?

I am merely concerned for my son's happiness, you see. As a wife should be for her husband's.

For his happiness... I understand.

Excellent! Now, we have a wedding to plan.

Siddhartha and Yasodhara had the most opulent wedding Kapilavastu had seen in many years.
Siddhartha never failed to be captivated by Yasodhara's kindness and humor.
My Gods, you're perfect. I wonder why I ever felt unhappy.
Oh, Siddhartha! You're not so bad yourself--
WOAH!
--but you can be a little clumsy!
THUD!
Oh, did we fall off the rooftop? I hadn't noticed.

Their love flourished for thirteen years. But eventually, Siddhartha once again began to wonder what lay beyond his palace walls.
Go back to sleep, my love.
Siddhartha?

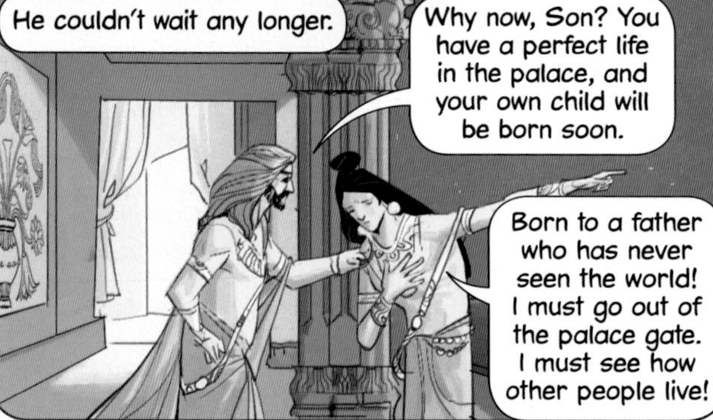
He couldn't wait any longer.
Why now, Son? You have a perfect life in the palace, and your own child will be born soon.
Born to a father who has never seen the world! I must go out of the palace gate. I must see how other people live!

Very well. You may take your chariot into the town today. I will make the arrangements.
Thank you, Father!

Act quickly. Send all available guards into the town...

'...Have them remove the elderly and infirm from sight...'

'...and let the people know that anyone who shows any sign of unhappiness will face my wrath.'

I've never seen a Prince before! What do you think he looks like?
He won't just be pretending to be happy and healthy, that's for sure.
Shh! Here he comes now.

Prince Siddhartha!
Everyone is so cheerful here. What a lovely life they must lead!
Good day, Your Highness!
Such a beautiful chariot!

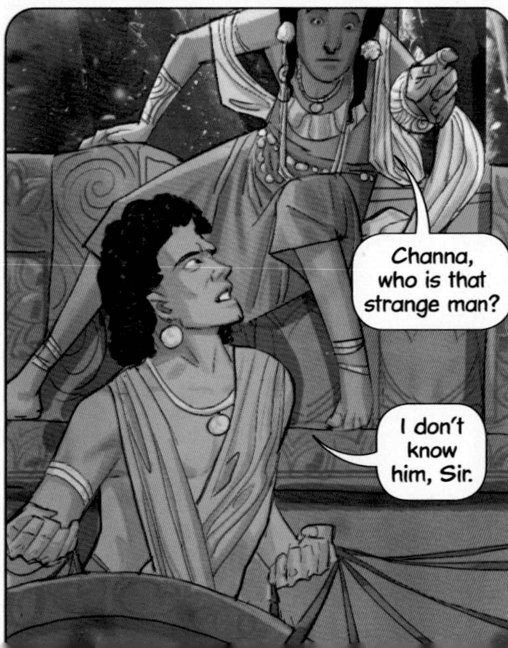

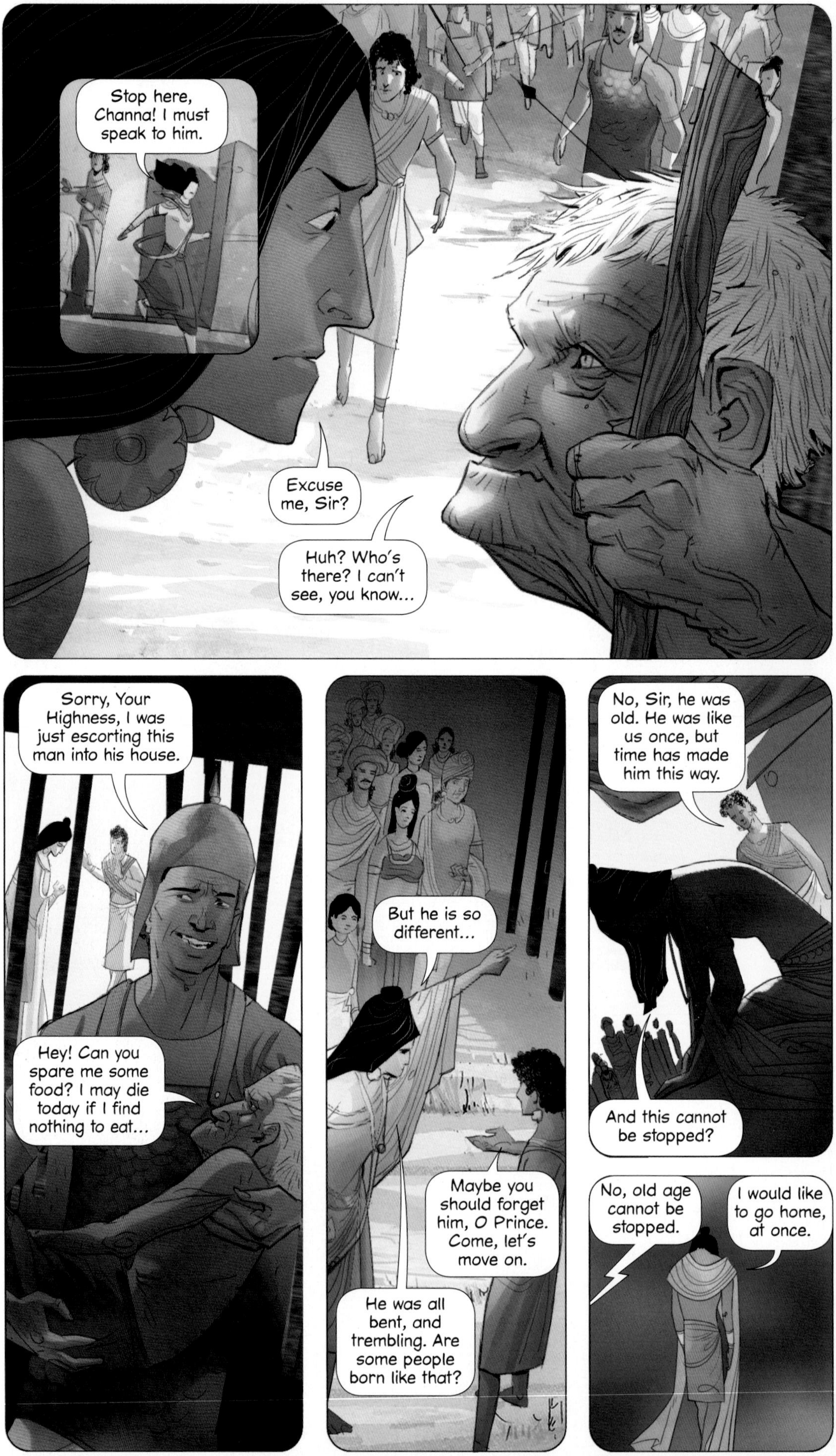

Stop here, Channa! I must speak to him.

Excuse me, Sir?

Huh? Who's there? I can't see, you know...

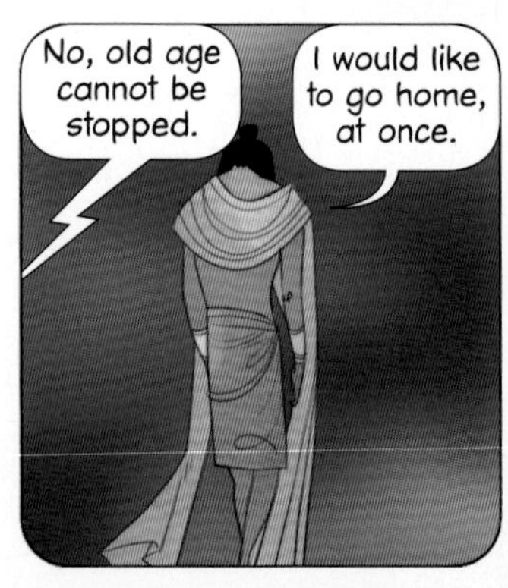

Immensely troubled by what he'd seen, Siddhartha did not sleep that night.

Siddhartha!
Father.
I've heard what happened in the town. You saw an old man, so what? You will live a long and luxurious life in the palace.

How can I enjoy that life, knowing what will become of me and of everyone I hold close?
Siddhartha, stop worrying and come to bed.

You, too, wish to keep me locked up here! You think it will keep me happy, do you?
I don't want to come to bed. I want to go into the town again, and not when the people wait in parade for me.

I must go and think this over some more.

See what you have done by sheltering him?
I can't let that blasted worrier leave the palace again! I shall have the guard increased!

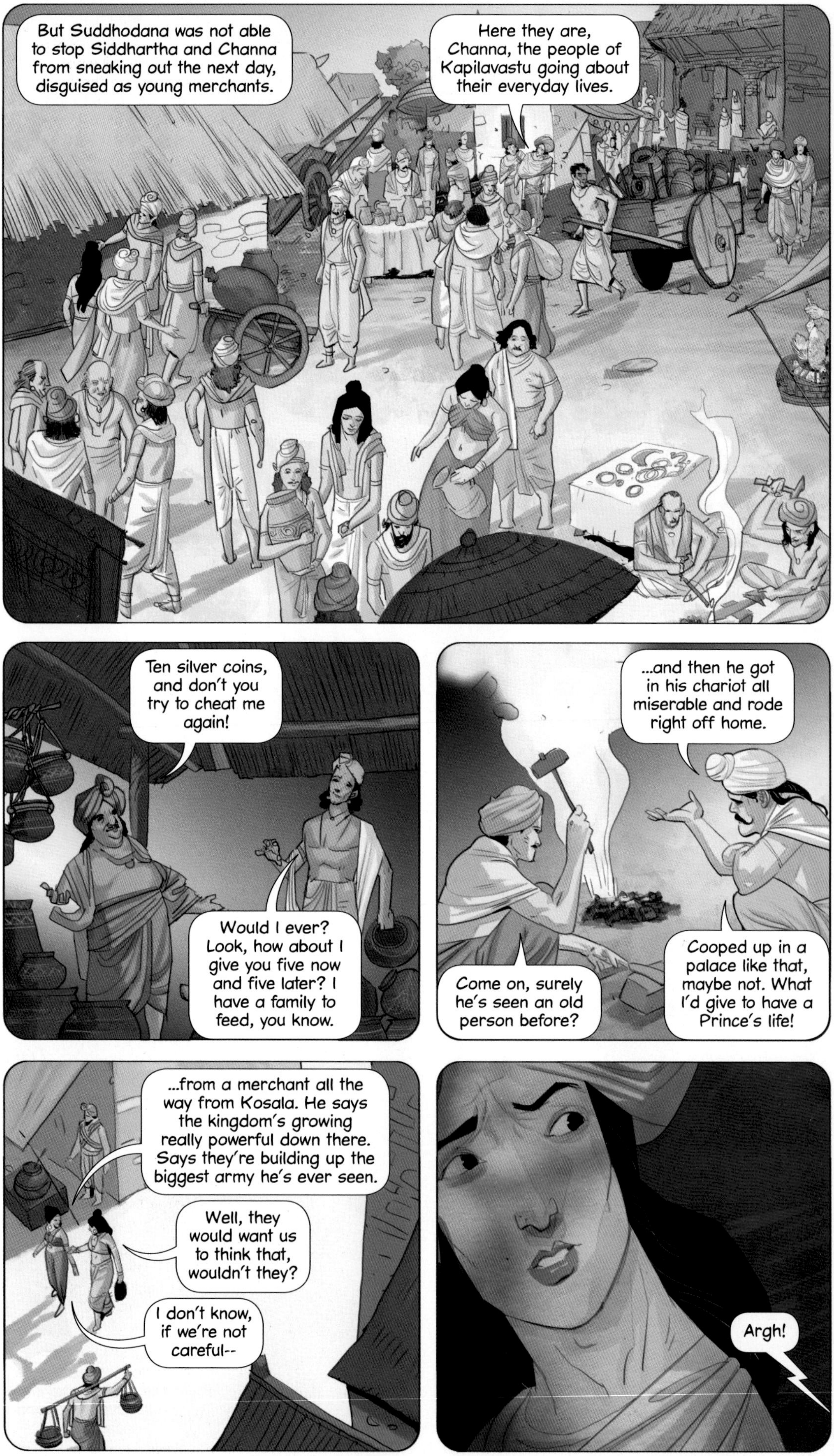

But Suddhodana was not able to stop Siddhartha and Channa from sneaking out the next day, disguised as young merchants.

Here they are, Channa, the people of Kapilavastu going about their everyday lives.

Someone needs help!

What is wrong with you?
Uhhh...

Channa, what's wrong with this man? Why can't he speak?
Don't touch him, Prince. He's sick! A horrible fever is burning his body!

Sick? Are there more men like this?
Yes, and you'll be next if you hold him so closely!

This can happen to anyone?
Anyone, at any time. No one can stop it.
Anyone can fall ill and suffer at any time...

Siddhartha reflected for days on the man's suffering. He had to know more about life in the town.
His third visit also ended depressingly...

No! Stop! What are you doing?

My Prince, please, let them!
But why does that woman lie so still? Why does she allow these people to burn her?

She is dead, Prince. Her soul has left behind an empty body.
Dead? Channa, does everyone die?
Yes. All living things must die. There is no escaping death.

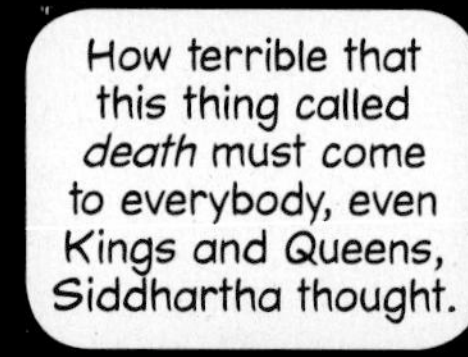
How terrible that this thing called *death* must come to everybody, even Kings and Queens, Siddhartha thought.

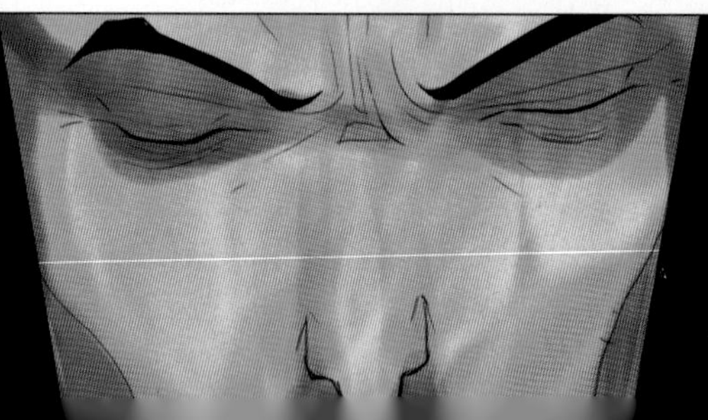
There must be a way to stop it. And he must find that way.

This is what spiraled around his mind as he sat alone for the next few days.
King Suddhodana, aware of Siddhartha's depression, had run out of options. Falling into despair of his own, he gave up on trying to keep his son inside.
But what Siddhartha saw on his fourth visit changed his perception on everything.
Tell me, Channa, who is that man in the yellow robe? He looks so contented.
He is a *bhikshu*, a monk. He goes from house to house to beg for food and travels the land teaching how to be peaceful and good.
A bhikshu... Perhaps I should be like him. Maybe that would help me end suffering. Come, let's talk to him.
Prince Siddhartha!
Prince! Magnificent news! Your child has been born! You have been blessed with a son!
Oh, that is such good news, my Prince!
A son...

Siddhartha! Come and see your son!

Are you not happy?

A feast was held to celebrate the birth... In truth, a last-ditch effort by Suddhodana to cheer his son up.
And Siddhartha, in truth, only attended to please his father.

Siddhartha! Cheer up, Cousin! You have a son!
The son will merely get in the way of me leaving this life and ending suffering, Devadatta. That's why I have named him *Rahula* – impediment.

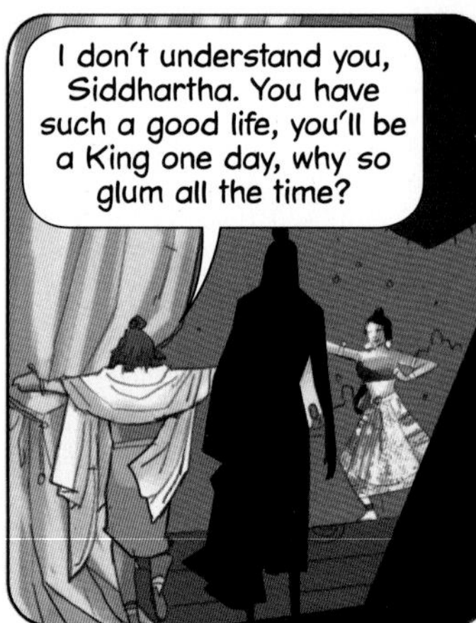
I don't understand you, Siddhartha. You have such a good life, you'll be a King one day, why so glum all the time?

...the guests had left, and the performers had fallen asleep.

He found the sight loathsome. He had to leave this stifling life, now!

Are you... Are you sure you want to leave like this?

I have to, Channa. My life is outside the palace now.

Then take me with you!
TLOT
TLOT
TLOT

This is where you leave me, Channa.

But, my Prince, I can be of use to you in your travels.

I am your Prince no more. I am a bhikshu, and I lead a simple life.

It's no use me living in the palace without you! I want to follow you!

Who's there?
Become a bhikshu, renounce the world, live a life of ordeals. You think you'll end suffering by begging for scraps?
Who are you?
I am a King, a great Lord!
As could you be if you weren't so damned intent on giving it all up.
I have to give it all up. I have to... to find a solution to suffering.
Tell me, Siddhartha Gautam, were you to be a great King, how would you rule over your people?
I would be a benevolent ruler. I would provide well for my people and would not force them into war.
Now that sounds like a good society to live in! And tell me, would your people suffer?
I would do my best to keep them from suffering, but--
Then you'd be a better King than many! Come on, Siddhartha...
...go back to your palace, back to your beautiful wife and newborn son...
...in one week you could become a Chakravarti. You could rule the world!

I could rule the world...
...But the world would still suffer. No King can stop old age, or illness, or death.
Pain cannot be conquered by force. No. I will be a bhikshu.
A bhikshu! Don't you want to feast on magnificent meats? Hoard all the riches in the world? Feel your wife's lips upon your own? Just desire it, and all that is yours.
I will be a bhikshu.
Very well. Live your silly simple life. But know this...
...One who should be a Chakravarti cannot live an utterly pure life, and one day, you will have an unkind thought, or a greedy one, or a spiteful one...
...And I'll be watching.

And so, as the sun rose over the River Anoma, Siddhartha began his wanderings of the world, seeking one who could teach him the ways of a bhikshu.
But this wasn't such a joyous day for everyone.
No... My son. I have failed.
I must find him. I must bring Siddhartha home. I will!
I don't doubt you, my King. But until then, do not worry, his place in the King's court will easily be filled.

2 THE LONG ROAD TO ENLIGHTENMENT

KNOCK!
KNOCK!

KNOCK!
KNOCK!

KNOCK!
KNOCK!

Siddhartha Gautam?
You are requested in the court of King Bimbisara.

My people speak of a young man known as Gautam who begs in the streets.
Tell me, are you the same Gautam who is sought after by the emissaries of King Suddhodana?
I am, Your Majesty. King Suddhodana is my father, but I have given up the princely life.

Why would you do that? Have you quarreled with your father? A man like you could make a fine ruler. Stay here and I shall give you half of my kingdom!

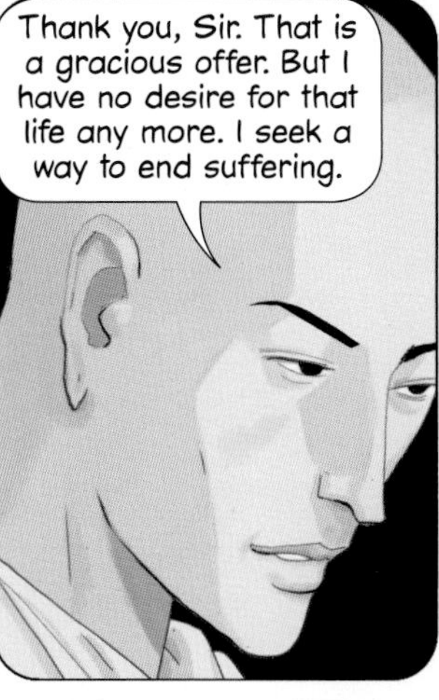
Thank you, Sir. That is a gracious offer. But I have no desire for that life any more. I seek a way to end suffering.

Ah! A spiritual man! Very interesting. You need to find a great teacher. I hear Alara Kalama is teaching in Vaishali.

Thank you, Sir. I will seek him out.
Promise me one thing, Siddhartha Gautam, should you find the enlightenment you seek, come back to Rajgir and preach to my people.
I would be honored to, O King.

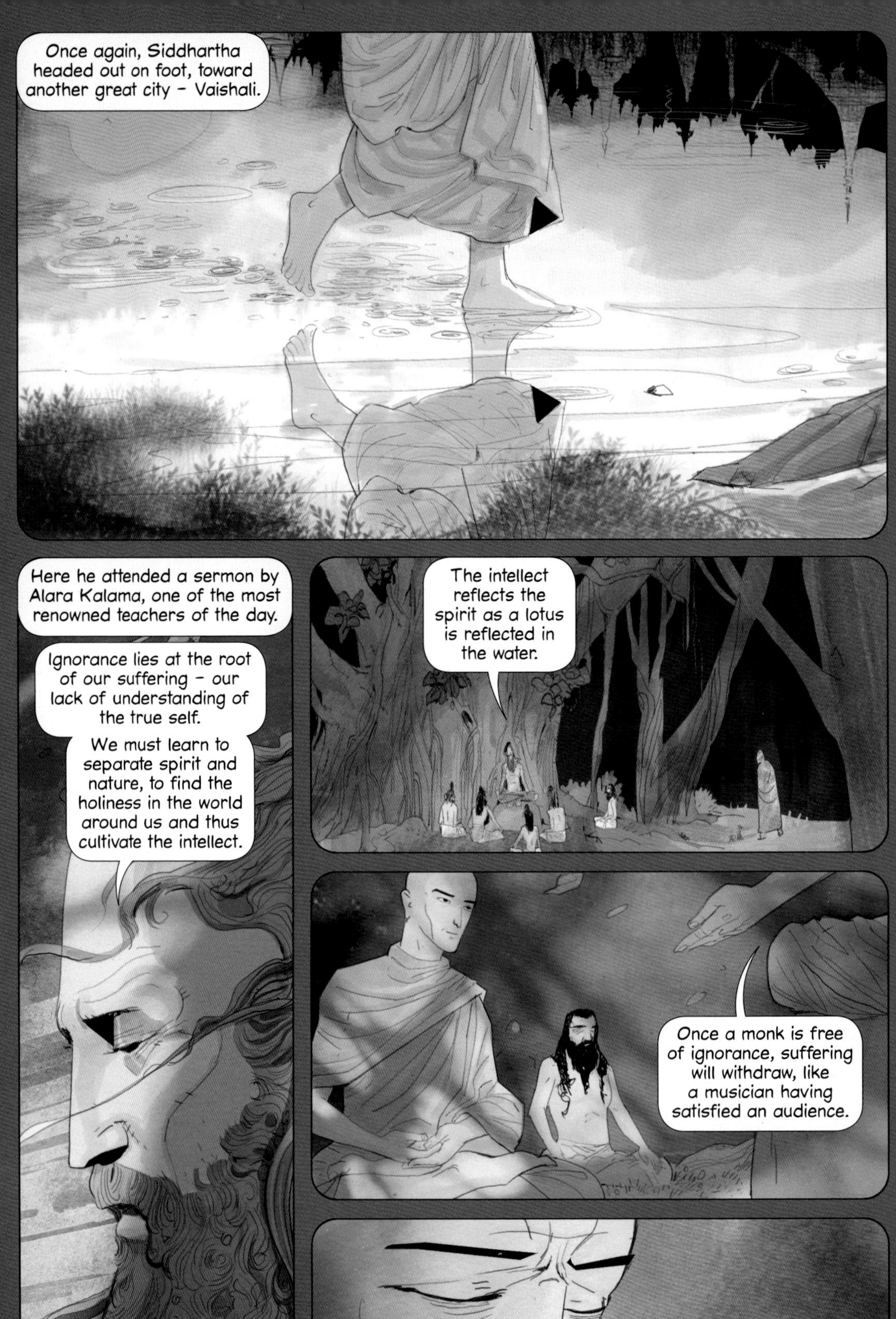
Once again, Siddhartha headed out on foot, toward another great city – Vaishali.
Here he attended a sermon by Alara Kalama, one of the most renowned teachers of the day.
Ignorance lies at the root of our suffering – our lack of understanding of the true self.
We must learn to separate spirit and nature, to find the holiness in the world around us and thus cultivate the intellect.
The intellect reflects the spirit as a lotus is reflected in the water.
Once a monk is free of ignorance, suffering will withdraw, like a musician having satisfied an audience.
Siddhartha was intrigued by Alara Kalama's ideology, his *dharma*, but not convinced. Something was missing.

I have learned all your sermons, Teacher, and yet they remain somehow... abstract. Not useful.
Do you doubt the truthfulness of my teachings, Siddhartha?
In a way, yes. I would like to know how you came across them. Surely you've not just taken someone else's word for all this?
I came across them through the disciplines of yoga, disciplines which I think you are ready to learn.
Alara taught Siddhartha the yogic disciplines: A position of perfect stillness, slowing of the breath, unwavering concentration.
He reached the joyous state he had first experienced as a child at the plowing ceremony, and after that, the freeing state of 'Nothingness'.
And yet, when Siddhartha left his trance, he was once again human. Once again prone to suffering.

You're telling me you've achieved Nothingness? Remarkable! I've never seen a student learn so fast!
Yes, but when I leave the trance--
You must lead my sangha with me! Be my partner!
But when I leave the trance, nothing has changed. I will still grow old, fall ill and die. Can your methods stop that?
Well...
They cannot. I will seek an eternal solution elsewhere.
Thank you for everything, Master Alara, and goodbye.

In his travels, Siddhartha heard of another teacher, Uddaka Ramaputta, who had developed an even greater form of yoga.
But the same cycle repeated itself. Siddhartha soon mastered Uddaka's techniques...
...only to remain dissatisfied.
Old age, sickness, death, will yoga ever solve these? How can it be done?
I know of no way to achieve what you seek, Siddhartha, nor do I know of anyone who can find a way.
There must be a way!
Once again, Siddhartha left his teacher behind.

An encounter with a familiar face* showed him another way of seeking the truth.
Who's there, under the water? Kondanna? Is that you?
Kondanna! Do you need help?
*See page 10
Kondanna! Are you OK? It's Siddhartha Gautam, you know my father!
Yes, I know who you are. I've known you since you were a baby. But I don't appreciate being interrupted.
You were drowning!
I was carrying out an ordeal!
A what?
An ordeal, subduing the body in order to expunge sin.
Come...

'...let me introduce you to my group.'
Friends, Siddhartha here wishes to know more of the ascetic lifestyle.
The material form is an obstacle to enlightenment.
Society is corrupt and obsessed with material pleasures.
Hence we put our efforts into subduing our bodies.
Only through rejecting the luxury of the physical self can we achieve liberation.
Interesting... Through the complete opposite of the noble lifestyle, you seek truth.
Will you join us, Siddhartha?
Yes, I will try your methods.

And try their methods he did. Siddhartha spent cold nights outdoors without clothing.
He held his breath for longer than he thought possible.
He lay on a bed of thorns.
And he fasted, eating as little as a single grain of rice a day.

Siddhartha took the ascetics' methods to extremes even they had not managed to.
But, as he became respected by the group, his health became perilously fragile.
His skin withered and his bones stuck out...
Until one day, Siddhartha's body could take no more punishment...

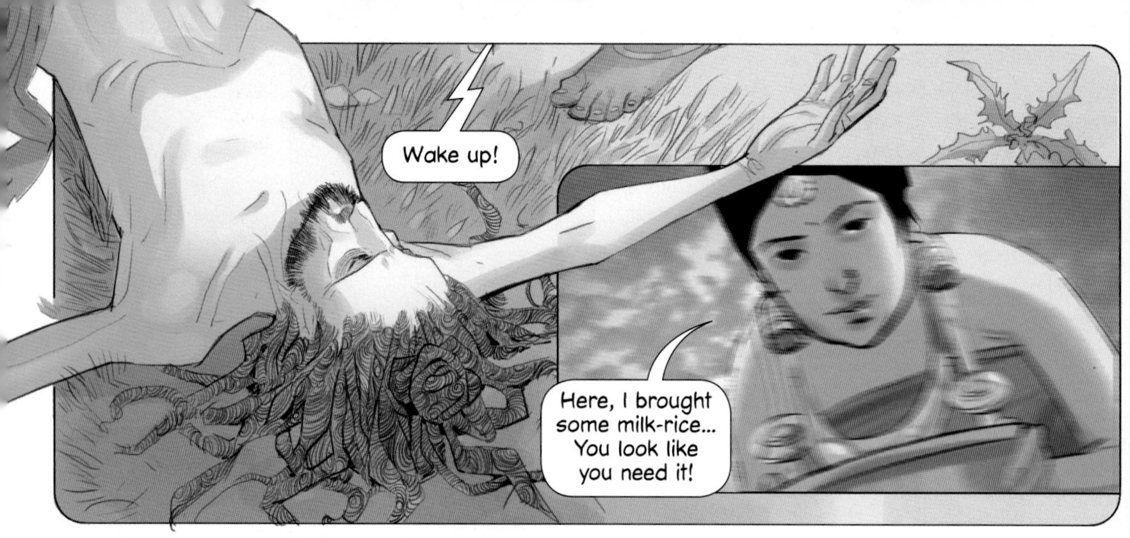
Wake up!
Here, I brought some milk-rice... You look like you need it!

What happened?
I saw you faint. No wonder, you're so thin.
Thank you for the food, but I can't take it, I'm...

Look, you'll die if you don't eat!

No, you're right. I do need to eat.

Mmm... This is good.

Siddhartha would never eat a full bowl!
That's unacceptable!
And behind our backs, too! He calls himself an ascetic!
We can't let him stay!
I suppose, if it is true... Yes, we must kick Siddhartha out of the group.
There's no need to, Kondanna.
I will be leaving you today.
For six years, I have tortured my body in search of the answer to suffering, and have found nothing but more suffering.
Asceticism is as fruitless as extreme yoga.

All the accepted methods of seeking enlightenment had failed Siddhartha.
He resolved to rely on his own insights from here on. How could he find the truth without following the ways of others?

And then, he was reminded of the insects at the plowing ceremony.
He was reminded of a joyous day on which he had achieved a meditative ecstasy without any effort, and without need for self-torture.

He realized that by working with nature, not against it, anyone could achieve enlightenment.
And he would do just that.
He chose a nearby tree. This would be the place.

But as Siddhartha approached the tree, he found the ground shaking under his feet.
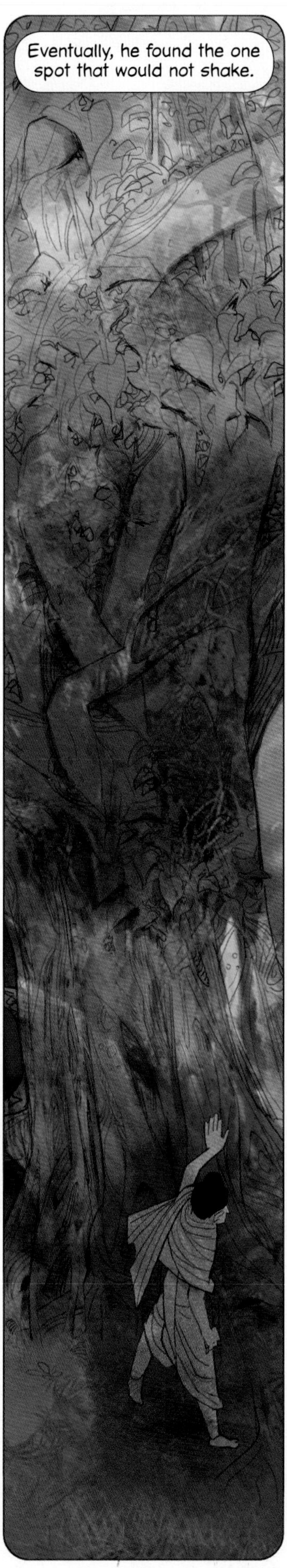
Eventually, he found the one spot that would not shake.

The immovable spot on which he would attain enlightenment.
But he was not yet free of material desires that could hold him back.
My, what a handsome King!

I am no King.
Oh, but you're noble enough to be one.
And strong enough.
And handsome enough.
You think yourself free of human folly.
Free of sin, free of desire.
But can anyone be? Really?
And why would you want to be? That's not exciting at all!
You... Who are you? You resemble Yasodhara...
I can resemble whoever you want me to, Siddhartha. A Chakravarti King deserves anyone he wants.
No! Leave!
You don't like me?
I loved Yasodhara very much... But I cannot allow myself sensual desires. Not any more.
You reject my daughters, Siddhartha?

And I was so looking forward to the wedding!
Hello, again. Is the army meant to frighten me?
The army is yours. Or, at least, it could have been had you chosen to be a King. Instead, it's mine! So, does it frighten you?
It does, doesn't it?
Wait until you see what they can do--
ATTACK

The collective armies of the demon Mara focused all their might upon Siddhartha.
But, when he did not fear them, their weapons could do no damage.

Siddhartha weathered nine storms unleashed at him.

You resist my army's attacks? Well done, very good.
But still, you must give up that spot. For I, the Mara, am a Chakravarti, and I should sit at the center of the world.
You do not deserve this spot, Demon. You are full of rage and violence. You have never performed any spiritual or compassionate deeds.
Oh, but I have. Haven't I, army?
He has!
We'll vouch for the Chakravarti Mara.
And what about you, lonely bhikshu? Who will bear witness to all these compassionate deeds of yours?

RUMBLE!!!
What? How can you--?
The Earth will be my witness.

Having conquered his inner demon of fear and desire, free from all that which kept him from the truth, Siddhartha meditated through the night.
He saw how this desire had been the cause of his suffering, and he understood how to be released from it.
He saw all his former lives - as animals, humans, and gods - pass him by, and he saw that this would be his last.

He saw the Earth, all the worlds of the Cosmos, and the landscapes of Heaven and Hell.
He understood the cycle of birth and death and he found the peace of Nirvana.
He found enlightenment.

3 BIRTH OF THE SANGHA

Having found enlightenment through his own insight, Siddhartha was now a Buddha.

He set out, intent on teaching his new discoveries.

Siddhartha? Is that the bhikshu Siddhartha?

It is a lot to take in... Maybe people will never believe me. Maybe it's not worth trying to teach.
No, you must!
Lord Brahma!
I saw you achieve Nirvana. What you've learned could change the world.
Not if people won't believe me.
Find people who will let you speak, and they will believe. Please, Buddha. The human race drowns in pain, many are in need of your teachings!
Travel far and wide. Save them.
Yes. I will teach my dharma...
...and I know just where to start.

The rain's clearing up.
Shame. I was hoping to sleep in it tonight.
Hey, look who it is!

Gautam, the luxury-lover who abandoned us!
No-one speak to him. He does not deserve our respect.
Wait... Do you not see something is different about him?
Well, he's put on weight.

Siddhartha! Welcome. You have changed.
Hello, Kondanna. Yes, I have found enlightenment! Would you allow me to preach to you my new dharma?

Enlightenment? After abandoning our ways? This can't be.
I think Kondanna may be right. He does look... somehow majestic. Let's hear him speak.

Friends, when leaving your noble lives, you rejected sensual pleasures. For this you must be commended, as a life of pleasure-seeking cannot lead to Nirvana.
But instead you have devoted yourselves to a life of self-mortification. This too is unhelpful and will not lead to Nirvana.
No, to become *arhats* - enlightened ones - you must follow a Middle Way.
There are Four Noble Truths that will help you follow this path.
First, this world is full of suffering.
Second, the cause of suffering is desire.
Third, the end of suffering, Nirvana, can be achieved by letting go of desire.
Fourth, the way to let go of desire is through following the Eightfold Path.

And so the Buddha had his first five followers.

No, I'd like to hear your story.

Oh. OK. My name is Yasa.

'I am the son of a rich merchant from Varanasi, but I have fled from the city. I'm fed up of the vanity and opulence of it all.'

Ah. I did a similar thing once, and have since found an end to any suffering.

Really? Could you teach me?

Of course. Come with me, and you shall learn.

I just couldn't take it any more, you see. I just had to leave, and--
Wait here. Something's wrong.
We haven't seen him.

I know my useless idiot of a son has come this way! Tell me where he is!
I told you, we haven't seen him!

Be hidden. I'll deal with this.

Sir. Indeed, your son has passed through these woods. We will help you find him, but first, please, sit down. I have much I would like to tell you.

What are you, some kind of a great teacher? With a sangha of *five*?
It is small, yes, but please, listen to what I have to say.
Now, the world is full of suffering...
And while the Buddha recounted his dharma to the rich merchant...
...Yasa listened in and became the Buddha's sixth enlightened disciple.
...the way to overcome desire is through the Eightfold Path...
Impressive! I've never heard a clearer dharma! To think I doubted you!
And now you may see your son again.
Yasa! What a teacher you've found! Now, come home. We can tell everyone in Varanasi of this Buddha.
Father, I, ah...
Sir, your son is now a bhikshu. The busy householder's life would no longer be appropriate for him.
Ah... Well, at least he is following a truly great teacher. Please, come and dine at my house.

The teachings soon spread. Nobles and priests from Varanasi and the surrounding countryside flocked to see the teacher Yasa now followed.

After a short space of time, the Buddha's sangha grew to sixty followers.

It is time for us bhikshus to spread out into the land...

'Go now, and travel for the welfare and happiness of the people.'

'Meditate on the holy life and teach the dharma.'

'You will find people who will understand it.'

'Of that I am sure.'

Who's this who enters the sangha of the Kassapa brothers?

I am a Buddha, Sir, traveling to spread my dharma.
A Buddha? Ha! And how many followers do you have, then?
Sixty, Sir, but--
Sixty? Do you know how many followers I have? Eh? One thousand!
And what dharma do you teach your one thousand?
We worship the sacred flame.
Hmm... My discourse is very different from your fire-worship. Perhaps some of your followers would like to hear it?
You think yourself enlightened like me?
I have reached Nirvana, yes.
Then demonstrate your powers. Move that top log with your mind.
What has that to do with my teachings? A superficial magic trick!
Making excuses, 'Buddha'?

Fine.
RUMBLE!
Hmm... Not bad.

You are a powerful bhikshu, I see. But you are no Enlightened One.
One more test. Read my mind.
It does not take a Buddha to do that, Kassapa. You believe yourself an arhat and I a pretender.
But you are wrong. One so egotistic as you can never achieve enlightenment.
How dare you insult me so? Your doctrine will never match up to mine! I will not discuss this any further!
Very well. If I may make one request, could you give us a place to rest for the night?
All right. Your followers may sleep in the kitchens. And you, since you see yourself as so great...

Are you sure about this, brother?

Of course. That damn bhikshu deserves everything the serpent does to him. Trust me, he won't leave the fire chamber alive!

Oh, no,
no, no...
Yasa!
What are
you up to?
A serpent
demon! There's
a serpent in the
fire chamber!

Hiss
Go on. I give you permission to kill me.
Oh!

Those fakers have a surprise in store this morning!

WHAT?

Any serpent can be tamed, Kassapa, through compassion, a quality which you distinctly lack.

So he thinks he'll convert us all? That's quite the claim.
I don't know what to expect. Did you hear he tamed the serpent?
That won't be necessary, Kassapa.
Of course it will, the sacred flame is integral to our sermons!
Nonsense! No one can tame the fire serpent!
Quiet, the flame's lit, he's starting!
Everything is burning.

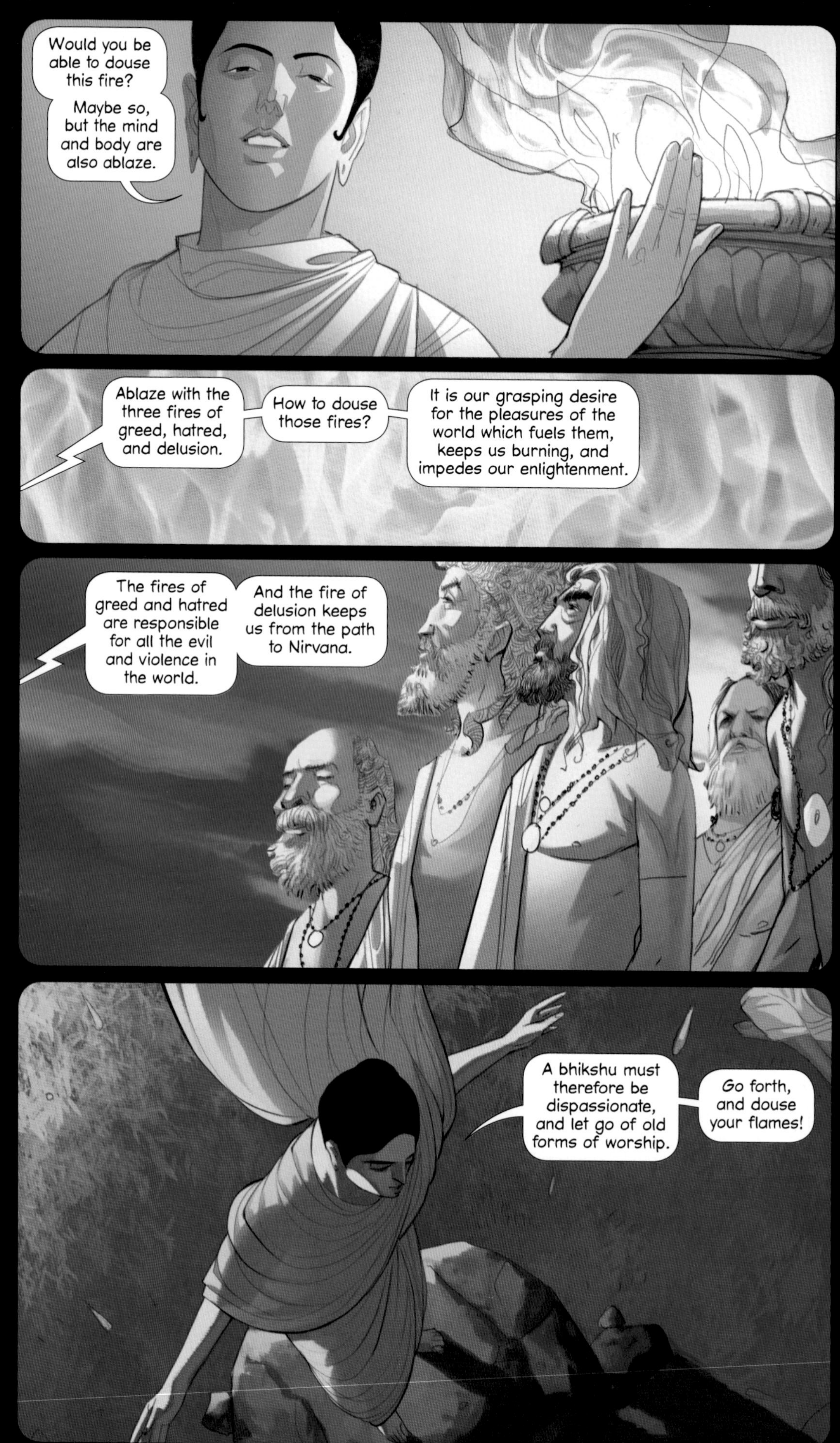
Would you be able to douse this fire?
Maybe so, but the mind and body are also ablaze.
Ablaze with the three fires of greed, hatred, and delusion.
How to douse those fires?
It is our grasping desire for the pleasures of the world which fuels them, keeps us burning, and impedes our enlightenment.
The fires of greed and hatred are responsible for all the evil and violence in the world.
And the fire of delusion keeps us from the path to Nirvana.
A bhikshu must therefore be dispassionate, and let go of old forms of worship.
Go forth, and douse your flames!

THUNDER
Buddha... Forgive me for my arrogance. Your sermons need no fire. I beg of you, accept me into your sangha.
The Buddha left the community with a thousand new followers.

It was with these followers that he returned to the city of Rajgir, to fulfill a promise made years before.
Let me through! I have an urgent message for the King!

This man claims to be a *Buddha*? I must meet him.
King Bimbisara!
Siddhartha Gautam, the Prince turned bhikshu! And Kassapa, the great teacher of fire-worship!
My apologies, but I'm unsure which of you is the teacher and which is the student.
Your majesty, I have abandoned fire-worship in favor of Master Gautam's teachings. He is truly a Buddha now.
A Buddha? Who can convert Uruvela Kassapa? What an honor! Please, dine in my palace today.

This Bamboo Grove has recently been completed. I want you to have it. Your sangha may use it however they wish when in Rajgir.

To think, not so long ago I was one of only five who followed you.
And before that, none did, and I wondered whether I'd ever be able to teach at all.
Will we stay under Bimbisara's hospitality for long, Buddha?
There are many yet to hear my teachings in Rajgir. Yes, I think this grove shall be our home for a while.
I can't believe this!
King Suddhodana must be told!

And what is it you wish to peddle to me this time, merchant?

Information, Your Majesty, I know where your son resides.

4 RETURNING HOME

During the Buddha's stay at the grove in Rajgir, the sangha flourished.
By chance, Sariputta, a member of another sangha known as the Skeptics, met the bhikshu Assaji in the street.
Excuse me, which teacher do you follow?
Oh, I've not followed him for long, I'm not ready to preach...
And yet you look like you've gained so much already! Please, I must know.
Sariputta immediately ran to pass this new dharma onto his friend Moggallana.
They soon joined the Buddha's sangha, and brought two hundred and fifty of the Skeptics with them.
Sariputta and Moggallana would become two of the Buddha's greatest disciples, Sariputta known for his wisdom and Moggallana for his miraculous power.

King Bimbisara regularly visited the Buddha for advice, which helped him rule the Kingdom of Magadha righteously.
But not all the citizens of Rajgir were enamored of the Buddha.
You dare turn my husband into a monk! Do you not think of the families?
First the Fire-Worshippers, now the Skeptics, who will you take next?
So many people against us, we need to do something!
Nothing more than we already do. In seven days or so, they will realize the virtues of our ways and the trouble will pass.
And indeed it did. When everyone had heard about the Buddha's dharma, he was the most popular teacher in the kingdom.

But in another corner of the land, he had not been forgotten.
Nine? Nine messengers have tried and failed to bring me my son?

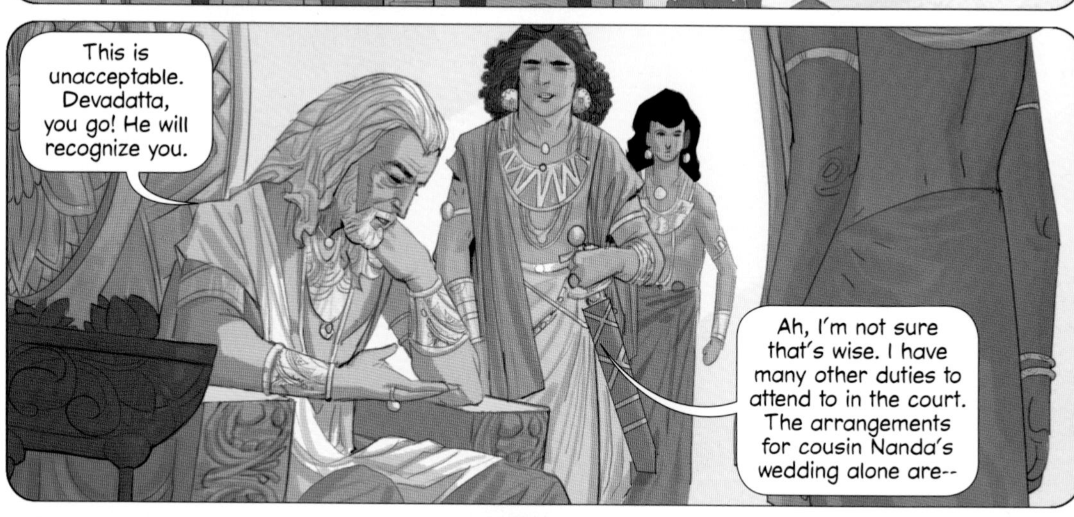
This is unacceptable. Devadatta, you go! He will recognize you.
Ah, I'm not sure that's wise. I have many other duties to attend to in the court. The arrangements for cousin Nanda's wedding alone are--

I'm Nanda's father, I can oversee the wedding.
With all due respect, Your Majesty, with your illnesses, I do not think that wise. Allow me to help.

I could go...
No, Ananda, you must help me here. May I suggest Kaludayi? He always got on very well with Siddhartha.

All right. Kaludayi, ride to Rajgir and bring back Siddhartha!

Siddhartha! Old friend!
Kaludayi! Come, dine with me.
You live in a park and eat scraps. This is so different from the palace life you could have had.
I no longer desire luxury. You wish to learn more about my lifestyle?
I am sure it is most virtuous, but maybe you can tell me more on the way to Kapilavastu.
Ah! So that is why you're here.
I bring a message from your father, old friend. He asks to see you.
Hmm...
Please, Siddhartha, he is old and growing ill.
Bhikshus, prepare to travel. We depart for Kapilavastu in the morning.

And so, for the first time in many years, the Buddha returned to his hometown.
Siddhartha!  
Devadatta. Ananda. How good it is to see you both!
Welcome back. Your father's health forbids him from seeing you at this late hour, but he will meet you tomorrow.

I can't wait to hear your teachings, Siddhartha. You must have gained so much wisdom.

Come now, Ananda, you have a great future in the palace court... Why bother yourself with spirituality?

Are you sure that's him?
That's him. I was here when he was Prince Siddhartha and he came to visit. He had a chariot back then.
Crazy, isn't it? He had the life of a Prince, and threw it all away.
I know. These nobles in their fancy houses, they think--
Careful.
SIDDHARTHA!
Father!
What do you think you're doing? Begging? In the street? How dare you insult your family name like this? You put me to shame!
I am not putting you to shame, O Great King. This is our custom.
Our custom? Nobody in our family has ever begged!
Not of the royal family, but of the Buddhas.
Huh! You wish to cut your ties with the family, eh? At least eat one meal in the palace with me.
That is not my wish at all. Let's dine together today, and I'll explain.

We'll need more seats over here. Let's get this place looking like the palace of Indra! And make sure Nanda and Janapada Kalyani's families get the best dishes.
Ah, Ananda! Did you check on the chefs?
Yes, yes, the deer's looking lovely!
And the invitations delivered to the so-called Buddha and his followers?
Yes, but... must you mock him?
A Prince should not lower himself to begging. It's shameful!
It's the path to enlightenment. I, for one, want to learn more about it.
Ananda... look over the feast we're preparing. Glorious, is it not?
It is very grand, yes.
This lifestyle was Siddhartha's once. He could have been a King. Instead, he wanders from park to park. And someone else will take Suddhodana's throne.
Nanda?
We'll see. Let's not forget I'm in the family too, and have served the court well.

...and through this method, desire is vanquished, suffering is eliminated, and Nirvana achieved.

I see. And this dharma of yours has helped people?
Yes. There are very few nobles or householders in Rajgir who have not learned from my doctrine.

I have educated the poorest soul in Magadha, an impoverished boy abandoned in a cremation ground.
And I have educated the richest soul, King Bimbisara, who uses my teachings to rule benevolently.

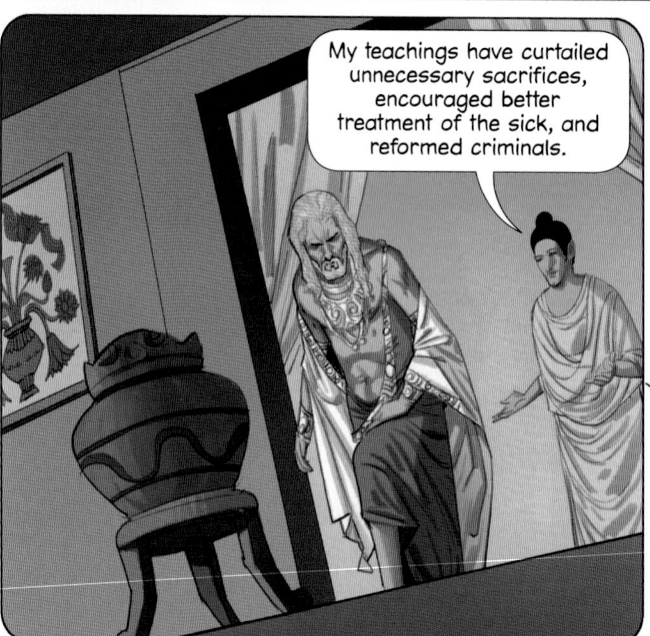
My teachings have curtailed unnecessary sacrifices, encouraged better treatment of the sick, and reformed criminals.

Come here.

All this could have been yours. It is a good kingdom, or at least I try to keep it so.

I won't pretend I'm not sad to have lost an heir. But... I now see how you've found something much more valuable.

That afternoon, the Buddha preached to King Suddhodana's household and gained many new lay followers.

Yasodhara. It's me, the one who was your husband.
My *husband*? Would a husband walk out on his wife in the night?
What I did was not done out of a lack of love for you.
Then why? Do you not remember the love you felt for me? Thirteen years we spent together!
I remember. But I have let go of that desire.
Well, it's not that easy for everyone to let go of desire. I remember our love every day, Siddhartha!
And every day I remember the pain of waking up to find you gone.
I can only apologize for the pain I have caused.
Rahula would like to see his father.

And so Yasodhara prepared her son to meet his father.
Remember, Rahula, your father could have inherited all of the King's wealth, but chose not to. He may not be the noble you're expecting.
Hey! You!
Rahula! How handsome a boy you are.
You're my father?
Yes.
But if you're from the royal family, why do you dress so plainly?
I've chosen a spiritual life, Rahula. I have no need for luxury.
Oh.
So... Does that mean I get all your palaces and money and nice clothes and...
You want your inheritance, do you? The only inheritance I have to pass on now is my teaching.
Oh.
That's rubbish.

This was inevitable.
Maybe one day Rahula will come to see the suffering inherent in the noble life, as you did.
Maybe. And maybe we should help him come to such a realization.
'Sariputta, your wisdom is undeniable, would you speak to my son for me?'
'He will be at my half-brother Nanda's wedding tomorrow. There should be ample opportunity at the feast.'
'It would be my pleasure, O Buddha.'

Congratulations on your marriage, Brother.
Siddhar... Buddha!
Hello again, Cousin.
I've been thinking... A life in the palace may be right for Devadatta or the King, but not for me. Could you tell me more of your dharma?
What do you want, you bald monk?
Your father tells me you want to live a royal lifestyle.
Yeah. I'll have lots of palaces and rule over all the kingdom, just like grandfather.
Rahula, look over there at your grandfather. He lives this life you seek, and yet is ill and old.
Wealth alone does not end suffering, but life as a bhikshu can.

Amazing! What you teach is so useful!
If you wish to learn more, Ananda, you would make a fine bhikshu.
Siddhartha! What do you think you're doing?
Stealing my brother away from the palace, are you? Don't listen to this fool, Ananda!
Devadatta, I do not mean to steal anybody. I was merely educating Ananda on a way to lead a better life.
A better life? In what way is your peasantry better?
You could have been a Chakravarti and ruled the world!
You could have stridden majestically through the skies!

You wish me to be a Chakravarti?

I am more than equal to any Chakravarti.

I am so sorry for doubting you, O Buddha!

We accept your power!

Please, Cousin, forgive me. Allow me to join your sangha.

The time came for the Buddha to end his visit. But first, he had a visitor...
Father!

Take me with you! I want to be a bhikshu.
You've changed your mind! Was it the levitation that impressed you?
No, it was Master Sariputta's words. I've been thinking about them over and over.
Very good. Sariputta, fetch a set of robes, you shall ordain my son!
Welcome to the sangha, Rahula!

Once again, the sangha traveled across the land... With a few new members...
Devadatta...
What do you want?
You were doing so well, Devadatta. You would have been a great King. Almost as good as you-know-who could have been.
But you've chosen a bhikshu's life, too? What does a demon have to do around here to find someone who actually wants power and glory?
I mean, there is still one other option. The Buddha's sangha...
The Buddha's sangha has the potential to hold more power than any Chakravarti.
Don't you worry, Mara, I'm well aware of that.

5 Rebellion
The next step on the sangha's journey was Sravasti, the most advanced city in the land and capital of Kosala, the most powerful kingdom.
Here, the Buddha found a park had already been prepared for them, by the merchant Anathapindika.
I heard you talk near Rajgir two rainy seasons ago, and have followed your dharma since. When I heard you were coming to Sravasti, I had to be the one to accommodate you, and this park was perfect!
But it was owned by Prince Jeta, who would only sell it to me if I laid all the grounds with gold, so I did just that!

Did you hear that Anathapindika plans to build a monastery for us right here?
Impressive...
Huh! I expected the sangha to be living far away in the forests. I never realized a spiritual teacher could command such influence.
Everyone's impressed when they hear the Buddha's dharma!
Even the wealthiest of merchants... Imagine what power that could bring us!
It's not about power, it's about spreading the dharma!
Oh, Ananda... Always the innocent one.

The Buddha and his sangha spent many seasons in Sravasti, residing in the newly-built Jetavana monastery.
But a terror plagued the nearby lands - the ruthless bandit Angulimala.
To pay off a debt, Angulimala had set out to kill a thousand people, and collect a finger from each.
King Prasenajit gathered his army to hunt down Angulimala, but hearing the sangha was nearby, wanted the Buddha's blessing before leaving the city.
Angulimala's mother took this as her opportunity. She'd find her son herself and convince him to stop killing.
But Angulimala was so determined to complete his thousandth kill that he'd slay even his own mother.

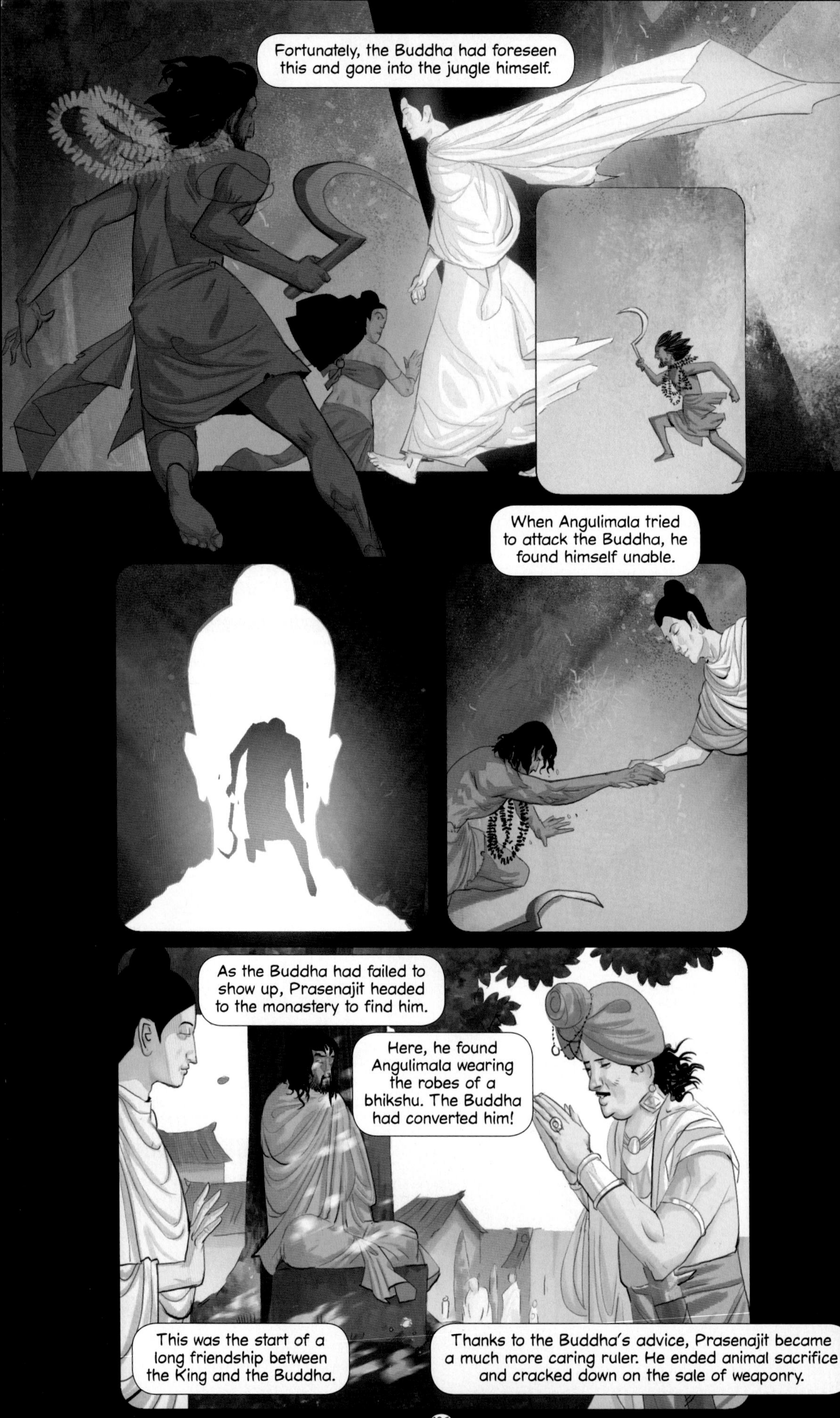
Fortunately, the Buddha had foreseen this and gone into the jungle himself.
When Angulimala tried to attack the Buddha, he found himself unable.
As the Buddha had failed to show up, Prasenajit headed to the monastery to find him.
Here, he found Angulimala wearing the robes of a bhikshu. The Buddha had converted him!
This was the start of a long friendship between the King and the Buddha.
Thanks to the Buddha's advice, Prasenajit became a much more caring ruler. He ended animal sacrifice and cracked down on the sale of weaponry.

During this time, the Buddha and Rahula returned to Kapilavastu once more, as King Suddhodana's illness had worsened.

He has lived a simple life these past years. He's truly followed your teachings.

My son... I have been happy, thanks to you. But now... now I fear death.

Father, look at the green leaves outside your window. Life continues. How can life and death bind us, when Rahula's body is also your body?

King Suddhodana achieved enlightenment on his deathbed.

The Buddha said one last goodbye to his father, and to Kapilavastu.

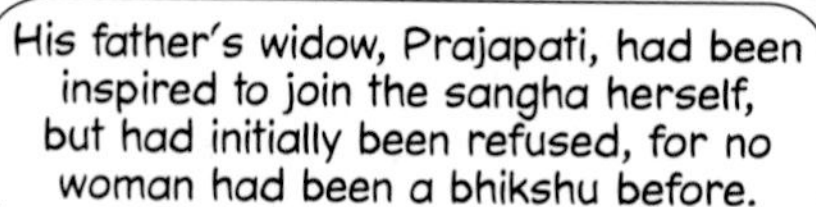

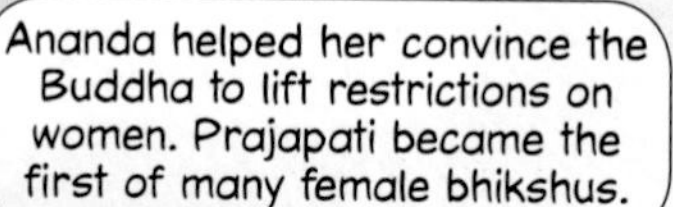

Ananda helped her convince the Buddha to lift restrictions on women. Prajapati became the first of many female bhikshus.

Rahula, meanwhile, was raised as a bhikshu, but could be as mischievous as any child.

His father's death had reminded the Buddha that he himself was getting older.
Before we leave Sravasti, it's time for me to appoint a personal attendant. Who volunteers?

I would be honored to, O Buddha.
As would I.
Sariputta, Moggallana, thank you, but your wisdom and talents will be useful elsewhere. I cannot take either of you as my attendant.
It should be me, Buddha. We've known each other since childhood, and with my experience in the courts, I could grant you informed advice.

What about you, Ananda?
Me?
I think you could make a fine attendant.

And so Ananda accompanied the Buddha as the sangha left Sravasti on their journey...

...a journey that would eventually return them to Rajgir, and to the hospitality of King Bimbisara.
I've missed your counsel, Buddha.
I like visiting your sangha. Everyone is honest and good-hearted. The grove is a peaceful place, a place of relief.
You seem weary, old friend.
It's the palace courtrooms... You never know who to trust. I can't walk through my own house without watching my back.
To be honest, O Buddha, I'm not sure how much longer I can manage as King--

'But I'm not sure whether my son Ajatashatru is ready to take the throne.'
It's not fair! I slave away in my father's court, and yet no one believes I'm capable of holding any authority!
I think you soon will be, O Prince.
After all, you'll soon be a father, why should you not also be a King?
Who are you?
I am Devadatta, my Princess. Formerly of the court of King Suddhodana of the Shakya. And I think your husband and I can help each other out.
Devadatta soon became Ajatashatru's trusted court bhikshu, and together they schemed... Devadatta would take control of the sangha, and use its influence to dethrone Bimbisara.

Devadatta built up allies among the younger members of the sangha, until he was in position to make his move.
Buddha!

Buddha, many bhikshus feel you are losing the energy of your youth and are no longer capable of leading the sangha. We ask that you step down, and allow me to take your place!
Brother, watch what you say!

It's all right, Ananda. What makes you think, Devadatta, that the sangha would fall apart without a leader were I to die today?
Every bhikshu is responsible for their own life. I pass on my teachings, but I do not dictate.
I would not allow Sariputta or Moggallana to take control of the sangha, never mind one as selfish as you.

Now, Devadatta, please leave the grove.

Devadatta could have been a wise bhikshu, but he let his ego get the better of him. There is no place for that in this sangha.
I'll ensure he is publicly dissociated from our order.

You failed? How could you? We're humiliated!
A setback. But we still have many supporters, in the sangha and in the city, too. The Buddha expelling me makes him look jealous.
Because you are a friend to me, and I'll be King!
Well, yes. But without control of the sangha, and with your father in good health, you will not be King soon. Except... There is another way.
Really? What are you proposing?
It's simple. We kill the Buddha.
KILL

'Kill him? How do we get to him?'
'You'll provide me with soldiers, O Prince. Or should that be... O King?'
'You'll soon have command of all the kingdom's armies.'
'But first, your father must die. And you must be the one to do it.'
'That way, everyone will see that you are ready to be King.'
Let me through!
Did he seem tense to you?

Father!
Oof!
THUD
A dagger? My Son, you wish to kill me?
!
My King, perhaps so bold an action suggests that Prince Ajatashatru is ready to take the throne... And to take the weight off your shoulders.
Hmm...
Very well. I knew my reign was coming to an end. I ask one thing of you, Ajatashatru, wear this crown with compassion.
Guards! Take my father to prison. Allow him no food. His weak leadership will never be seen again!
What? No! My Son, you can't do this!
I'm King now, Mother!

'I can do whatever I want!'
That's him! Ready?
Time to DIE!
Hey!
If you lay a finger on him--
Step down, Ananda.
Assassins, kill me if you will, but only if you believe it is the right thing to do.
This isn't right. I'm used to fighting armies, but killing an unarmed bhikshu...
Thank you. Stay on your guard, Ananda...

'...further attacks may be coming.'
Here he comes...
Push!
RUMBLE!
CRACK!
AH!
Buddha!
I'm all right, just a scrape.

Who do you think is behind these attacks?
It's Devadatta, I'm certain of it.
'My Brother! How can we stop him?'
'He won't keep his authority for long. Schemers like him never do.'
'Until then, we will weather his attacks.'
'There'll be more? What form do you think they'll take?'
Probably something like that.
STOP!

Three times you've tried to kill the Buddha, and three times you've failed.
My King, I...
Tell me, Devadatta, how much longer must this last?
One more attempt, O King, is all that is necessary. A larger troop of soldiers will infiltrate the Bamboo Grove, and...
And yet more of my soldiers will end up becoming his followers!
To be honest, Devadatta, I barely see the point any more.
I sit in the throne now. If you will keep failing me, I have no further need for your counsel.
My King, I must protest, it is I who helped you into the throne, and my wisdom can prove useful yet.
If you really are so wise, bhikshu, you'll leave this palace now, before you end up joining my father.
And stay away!

As Bimbisara languished in prison, his only blessings were the visits from his wife Kosala Devi.
Stop there.
What's this, then?
A present for us? Well, I am hungry.
My love...
I'm sorry. The guards found the food this time.
Oh, no... At least give me news, how does our son rule?
Ah. You won't like this, but... He rules aggressively. He has tried to kill the Buddha.
Maybe it is for the best that I rot in here. This way I don't have to see the mess Ajatashatru makes of my kingdom.

Ananda, something is bothering you.
It's nothing, O Wise One.
Please, we have a moment before my sermon, tell me.
Well, it's just... I'm struggling to understand why you chose me as your attendant.
Since you picked me, I've done nothing but fail you. I acted with aggression toward your attackers and I failed to pull you from the path of the boulder.
Ah, but you have never forgotten to wash my robe, or to tidy my quarters, and you have acted with humbleness and compassion for all, when Prajapati arrived, for example.
Yes, you have made mistakes, but unlike those with more ego, you ***understand*** that you have, and you will learn from your errors.
'I fear the same could not be said of your brother.'
'He would never serve well, as he desires to rule.'

Ah, just as I expected.
Hello, Buddha. I'm here to present my new rules to the sangha.
New rules?
Bhikshus! The Buddha proposes we follow a Middle Way between shameful indulgence and the true spiritual path. He proposes we accept corrupting luxuries into our lives!
No more! From now on, we shall live only in the forest, sleeping at the feet of trees. We shall wear only rags, and we shall refrain from eating anything not obtained through begging.
You know well my teachings about why such self-punishment is fruitless, Devadatta. The sangha will not accept these new rules.
The Buddha refuses! He is given over to luxury and self-indulgence! We must reject this corruption! Who is with me?
I am!
Let me join you!
And I!
What about you, Brother? Come, help me lead my new sangha.
No! My place is by the Buddha's side.
Hmm... You'll regret that when you've spent your life as a servant.

We've lost about five hundred bhikshus overall.
This is very troubling. They will live an unnecessarily harsh lifestyle, just because Devadatta craves power over them.
They were mainly young bhikshus, they hadn't heard all of your dharma yet, Buddha! If we send someone after them, we can win them back.
You're right! Sariputta, Moggallana, go at once!

Meanwhile...
You're clean. Go on through.
Shame.
Kosala Devi... I fear this will be the last time I'll see you.
Oh, Bimbisara, there's no need to be so down!
Is that honey? You bathed in honey?
I won't let you starve just yet.

You called for me, O King?
My guards tell me that the former King lives. And yet I have fed him nothing. Why could this be?
Your father is a strong man, my King.
Nonsense! You must be smuggling him food! And you know what my punishment is for those who consort with criminals?
Ajatashatru, please don't be so cruel to your own mother!
Huh! Fine. Mother, you may not make any further visits. Other than that, you will not be punished.
No! But losing my Bimbisara – your father – is the worst punishment!
Count yourself lucky. Guards, bring me my barber! I have a special task for him.

You've all made the right decision, bhikshus! Through following me, you will become truly enlightened!

Ah, the wise Sariputta and Moggallana! You wish to join my assembly?
Yes, Devadatta. We have deserted the Buddha.
The Corrupt One's two best disciples choose me over him! Brilliant! Sit, and hear me talk.

No longer shall his so-called Middle Way corrupt the minds of young people...

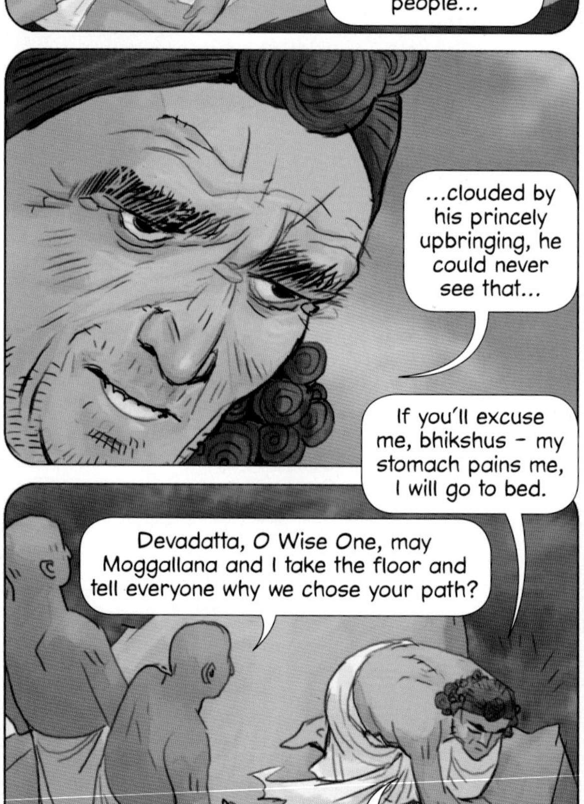
...clouded by his princely upbringing, he could never see that...
If you'll excuse me, bhikshus - my stomach pains me, I will go to bed.
Devadatta, O Wise One, may Moggallana and I take the floor and tell everyone why we chose your path?
Yes, good idea!

OK, he's gone.

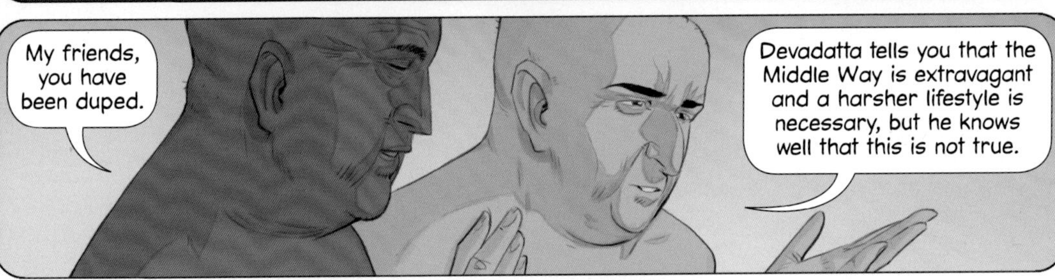
My friends, you have been duped.
Devadatta tells you that the Middle Way is extravagant and a harsher lifestyle is necessary, but he knows well that this is not true.

What? How can that be?
The Buddha himself lived an ascetic life for seven years and concluded it fruitless. This is core to his Middle Way: A bhikshu must keep his mind and body healthy to be able to act with compassion.

But why would Devadatta lie to us?
Devadatta was jealous of the Buddha. He would have said anything to get his own sangha.
For a man who now claims to believe in abstinence, Devadatta enjoys the luxury of power suspiciously much.

So, who will join us and return to the Buddha?
Now you mention it, he does seem a bit full of himself.
Tell us more of the Buddha's dharma!

What do you want, mother?
It's Vajira, she's having the baby!
Why didn't you tell me? I must see my child at once!
A barber? Has my son seen his folly and chosen to release me? A trim before I get out, is that it?
I have a son!
What a beautiful boy you are! I can't wait to pamper you with gifts fit for a Prince, to play games with you, to show you off to every visiting noble. We'll hold a festival so all of Rajgir can know about you!
Mother, did my father love me as much as I love my son?
You want to know if your father loved you?

'When you were born, a great Brahmin predicted that you would become your father's enemy. Many thought you should be killed immediately to protect the King, but he refused.'
'Do you see that scar on your thumb? That was a boil you had when you were small.'
'When your father heard you were crying in pain, he came running from his royal duties and sucked the pus from the boil himself.'
I can only hope that you will love your son half as much as your father loved you, for then he shall have a blessed life.
Oh no!
You! Stop! Don't carry out my order!
I'm sorry, my King, it's already done.
No! How could I do this? Gods, please forgive me!

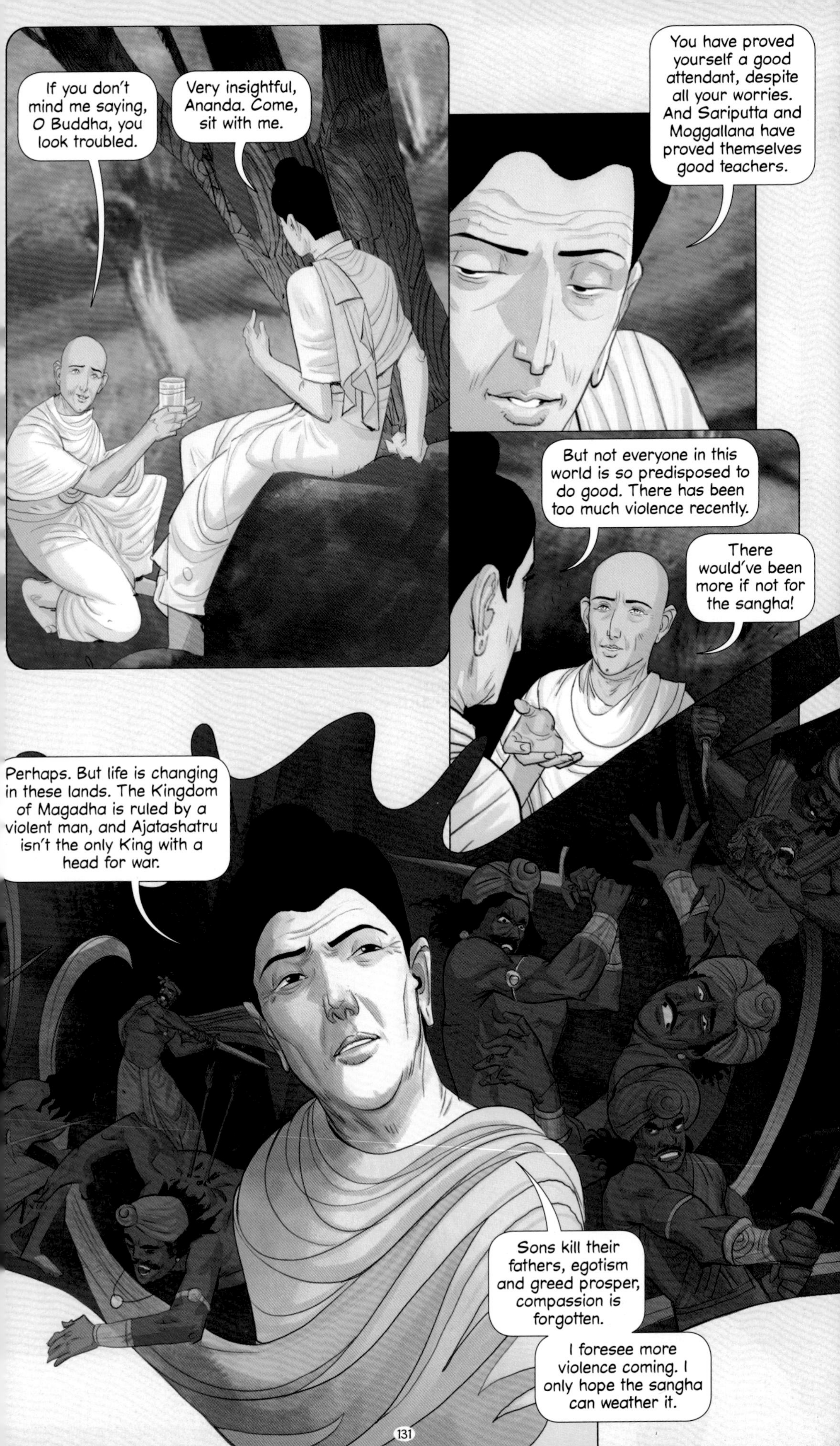

If you don't mind me saying, O Buddha, you look troubled.
Very insightful, Ananda. Come, sit with me.
You have proved yourself a good attendant, despite all your worries. And Sariputta and Moggallana have proved themselves good teachers.
But not everyone in this world is so predisposed to do good. There has been too much violence recently.
There would've been more if not for the sangha!
Perhaps. But life is changing in these lands. The Kingdom of Magadha is ruled by a violent man, and Ajatashatru isn't the only King with a head for war.
Sons kill their fathers, egotism and greed prosper, compassion is forgotten.
I foresee more violence coming. I only hope the sangha can weather it.

6 FINAL NIRVANA
The Buddha's fears were well-founded.
Though his teachings had spread much peace and goodwill, the increasing powers of the kingdoms meant increasingly bloody territorial disputes.
King Ajatashatru became a lay disciple of the Buddha and, from time to time, would ask him for advice.
But no advice would temper his war-faring instincts.
Ajatashatru led a bloody campaign against the Vajji Republics. His goal: Total extermination.

King Prasenajit of Kosala, himself tired of political egotism and infighting, took to riding out into the countryside to escape the courts.
One day, his General tricked him, abandoning Prasenajit in the countryside.
The King tried to reach his allies in Rajgir...
...but died a pauper's death along the way.

Like Bimbisara, the good King Prasenajit had been deposed by a greedy son.
King Vidudabha invaded the Buddha's homeland, executing many of the Shakya clan, regardless of age or gender.
The Buddha took this news silently.
He was growing old, and the world was changing... Not all for the better.
The Buddha decided to leave the cities and travel north, to preach in the marginal regions of the land.

He passed through the city of Vaishali, where the courtesan and musician Amrapali fed the sangha and gifted them her Mango Garden.
Here, the Buddha made a decision that worried some of his disciples.
Bhikshus. I wish you to stay in Vaishali and preach to the local population over the coming monsoon season. After that, spread out over the land.
But what will you do, O Buddha?
Myself and Ananda will travel further north alone. There are many villages where my teachings would be welcomed.

You're not well.
I'm well enough to carry on.
Sariputta and Moggallana are both dead.
My best disciples... gone.
But there is nothing to be feared in death. Sariputta and Moggallana were both arhats – they have found their Nirvana.
I understand, but...
But you are afraid I will soon die too, and you don't know who will lead the sangha?
Yes.
Do not fear. As long as my teachings are passed on, Ananda, the sangha needs no leader.

The Buddha weathered this monsoon in the village of Beluvagamaka. His health didn't improve.
Hello, old Friend. Wow, you are old!
What do you want, Mara?
Am I disturbing you? Sorry. A man your age needs his rest, right?
I mean, look at all you've achieved in your life. Despite all that nonsense I spouted about being a King, you showed me!
But that's all done now. Time for your final rest.
You deserve it.
Just close your eyes and drift away...
No!
Be happy, Mara, for I will be dead soon.
There is work still to be done.
Come, Ananda. Today we begin our journey back to Vaishali.
To Vaishali, Great One?
Yes. I must prepare the sangha for my death.

Bhikshus from the surrounding area gathered at the Service Hall in Vaishali.
This would be the Buddha's final sermon.
I just don't know how we'll keep going without him--
How will we keep ourselves organized?
Maybe his death will be a blessing, it could free us of his restrictions.
What do you mean? He's been a wise and fair leader!
Maybe he's going to put someone new in charge.
But who? With Sariputta and Moggallana gone too...
Looks like we're about to find out.
Bhikshus...

As I'm sure you have all heard, I will soon reach my final enlightenment, my Parinirvana.
After this, the responsibility for maintaining the sangha will not fall to a single central authority, but to each and every one of you.
Spread my teachings as far as they continue to be valuable, but do not assume that simply passing on my words is enough.
I have only taught what I have fully experienced for myself. Do the same, take nothing on trust, and make the dharma a reality for yourselves.
And above all, live for others.
The holy life was not devised for the sole benefit of the enlightened.
Live the dharma for the welfare and happiness of the people, out of compassion for the world.
That way, the sangha will live on through these troubling times.

Much of my life has been spent preaching in remarkable towns like Vaishali.

Eat up. I'm sorry it's no feast, but--

It is an excellent meal, Cunda. In times like these, eating with the son of a goldsmith can surpass eating with a King.

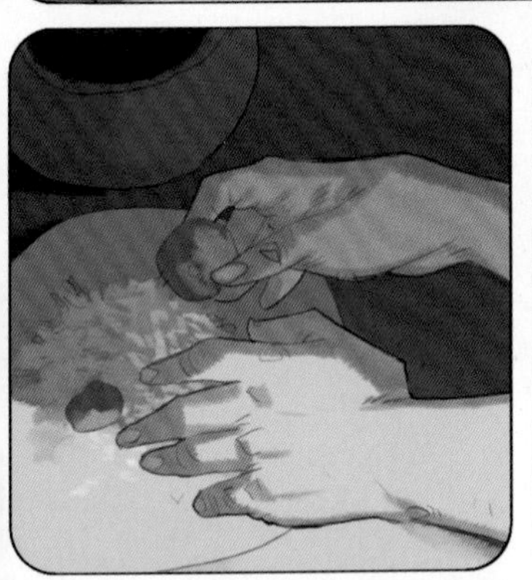

You're really ill! That food – it poisoned you!
COUGH!
Yes... I'm afraid you're right.
Come on. We're nearing the end now.
Here. Lay me a bed.
Ananda... If you ever see Cunda again, tell him he is not to blame for my death. It's a great honor to serve the final meal of a Buddha.

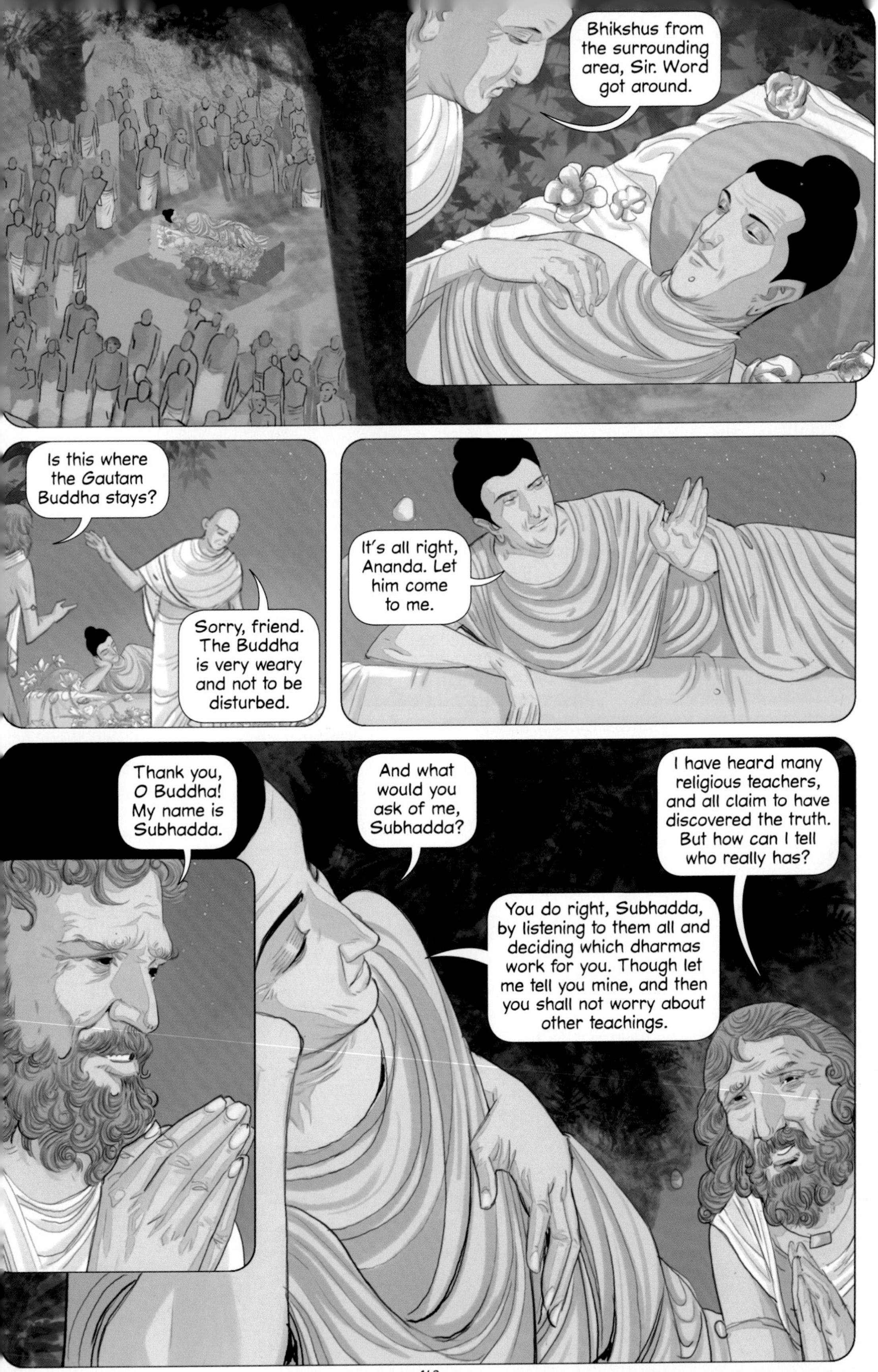

Bhikshus from the surrounding area, Sir. Word got around.

Thank you, O Buddha! My name is Subhadda.

And what would you ask of me, Subhadda?

I have heard many religious teachers, and all claim to have discovered the truth. But how can I tell who really has?

You do right, Subhadda, by listening to them all and deciding which dharmas work for you. Though let me tell you mine, and then you shall not worry about other teachings.

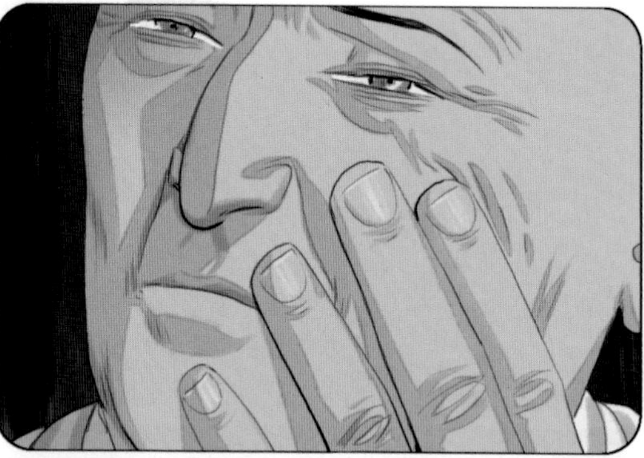

Oh, Ananda. You have been such a caring attendant. But you should not think in this way.

Bhikshus, I have passed on my dharma to each and every one of you, and have laid foundations for the sangha to survive should you maintain it.

If any of you has doubts about this, question me now.

Not a single one! That is wonderful!

Because all who practice my teachings are destined for enlightenment.

All individual things pass away. Work hard to gain your salvation.

The bhikshus knew now that they all had work to do in order to preserve the sangha.
A meeting was planned, which would gather together five hundred of the Buddha's followers.
Ananda knew that it would not be right to attend the meeting as a mere learner, and so practiced the Buddha's meditation techniques.
At the Sattapanni Cave in Rajgir, Kassapa presided over the First Buddhist Council.
But it was a newly enlightened Ananda that recounted and answered questions on the Buddha's dharma.

The sangha kept the Buddha's message alive across northern India for the next few centuries.
One of the most ardent followers of Buddha's message was the Emperor Ashoka, once a ruthless despot, who later had a realization of the suffering he had caused.
He converted to Buddhism and vowed to govern righteously, liberating slaves and building hospitals. He sent missions to spread Buddhist principles across Asia.
Throughout history, the sangha brought a degree of peace to war-torn lands...
...making Buddhism a truly global religion.